PRAISE FOR
A MILLENNIAL WORLD

"By growing up with dyslexia, Andrew has experienced what it is like to struggle with something holding him back, and yet he continued to push through to find something that he loves: entrepreneurship. A Millennial World shows just how much millennials—with diverse backgrounds—can learn and grow in today's age."

– SCOTT BARRY KAUFMAN, SCIENTIFIC DIRECTOR, THE IMAGINATION INSTITUTE AND AUTHOR OF *UNGIFTED: INTELLIGENCE REDEFINED*

"Andrew is one of the most well-connected seventeen-year-olds I've met in the last few years, and in A Millennial World he shares how he has been able to connect with so many people over his evolution of growing up. He shares how millennials have the ability to do everything he has done and more just by the power of technology, an advantage other generations weren't exposed to and didn't have access to."

– ABBEE PHILLIPS, PRINCIPAL AT JM SEARCH

"Andrew Rosenstein's understanding of millennials is as engaging as it is profound. For a generation growing up with constant technological disruption, low job security, and high economic uncertainty, they've all had to become entrepreneurs in one way or another—their entire professional lives becoming their own small businesses. A deeply thought-provoking read."

"Andrew is the true definition of an entrepreneur. I met him a few years ago at a networking event, and ever since he has never failed to impress me. A Millennial World shows the potential of such a powerful generation. It speaks not only to how millennials can be powerful but as well as how companies can take advantage of how smart and creative they are."

"Andrew understands how millennials work, buy, and communicate. A Millennial World offers valuable insights on how organizations can better prepare themselves for millennials to takeover!"

"After meeting Andrew, I realized how important it was for our company to figure out a strategy to market to millennials. They're an extremely important consumer group as well as an important part of the workforce. Andrew is an expert on millennials as he himself is one. My team and I very much enjoyed working with him as he really opened our eyes to the millennial generation."

"Andrew is an exceptional young person and entrepreneur whose work and knowledge are assets to anyone he engages with. He's been a part of our team at Glass-U for three years, and I'm privileged to have been a part of his growth and to have had him be a part of ours. A Millennial World touches on the power of what young people like Andrew can do."

"At Voxburner, our goal is to better understand the constantly changing strategies of youth marketing. Andrew worked with us to achieve this mission by bringing his unique millennial mind-set and experiences. I believe that companies can utilize A Millennial World to enhance their connection with this generation, which happens to have the largest spending power the world has ever seen."

"Finding your passion can be hard at a young age. Andrew has been able to not only find his passion, but he has also been able to find something that he loves and is good at. I believe that after reading A Millennial World, every millennial will be able to find their passion and mix it with a talent that they are good at to become successful. Andrew is an entrepreneur who is never scared to take risks, and this book proves that age and challenges should never hold you back from doing what you love."

– CAMERON HEROLD, FORMER CHIEF OPERATING OFFICER OF 1-800-GOT-JUNK AND BEST-SELLING AUTHOR

A MILLENNIAL WORLD

A MILLENNIAL WORLD

UNDERSTANDING the DRIVE
of a RISING GENERATION

ANDREW ROSENSTEIN

A MILLENNIAL WORLD

Understanding the Drive

of a Rising Generation

ISBN 978-1-61961-475-8 *Paperback*

       978-1-61961-476-5 *Ebook*

LIONCREST

PUBLISHING

For Mom, Dad, and Adam, for supporting everything I do.

CONTENTS

═══

OUR GREATEST STRENGTHS

DO A GOOGLE SEARCH for the term *millennials,* and here's what you'll find:

Millennials are lazy.

Millennials are weak.

Millennials are idiots.

Millennials are often seen as an entitled, snobby generation, always on our phones, constantly texting, posting, and tweeting. It is true that millennials are more connected on social media and other technology than previous generations. However, this not a disadvantage or weakness. It is a strength and just one of many that millennials possess. As more millennials start to enter the workforce and shape the future, I believe people will see that negative media depictions of our generation have underestimated us.

So what exactly is a millennial? The term typically refers to the generation born in the 1980s. Those born in the late 1990s through the early 2000s are sometimes called Generation Z. These groups, however, are essentially the same. They share similar traits, mind-sets, and benefits. For this reason, we'll simply use the term *millennials* to cover both.

Born in 1999, I grew up, like all millennials, immersed in digital technology and social media. At a young age, I realized I had a passion for entrepreneurship. While still in high school, I launched my first business ventures. I have been fortunate enough to see these enterprises succeed and grow. But it has not always been easy.

My family has a history of learning disabilities. My grandmother was dyslexic, although she was never formally diagnosed. My father had an auditory processing disorder. My brother is on the autism spectrum. At age eleven, I was diagnosed with attention deficit hyperactivity disorder (ADHD) and dyslexia, which explained why I had always struggled with reading and writing. I could read the words on a page but could not tell you what a book was about. This caused a lot of frustration and kept me from reaching my full potential.

Every day in elementary school, my class would read out loud. Each person would take a turn reading a page. While it took everyone else two minutes to read a page, it took me ten. Then, when they asked me what it was about? Forget it. I could not understand what I had read, so I made jokes out of it. Everyone laughed, but inside, I was not laughing.

After being diagnosed with dyslexia, I withdrew from my public school outside Philadelphia and enrolled in AIM Academy, an independent college prep school that specializes in students with language-based learning disabilities. Founded in 2006, AIM Academy focuses on students' strengths, empowering them to learn in a unique and effective way.

For example, we don't just read the fourth act of *Romeo and Juliet* and then take a quiz on it. Instead, we read the play, reread and discuss it, and thoroughly learn the text by acting it out. But rather than using Shakespearean language, we analyze scenes from the perspective of a present-day teenager. We ask ourselves how a fourteen-year-old *today* would respond to situations in the play, as opposed to a teenager from the Elizabethan age. This approach enables us to more fully comprehend the material.

Once I enrolled at AIM, I immediately saw an improvement in my learning. I was becoming more confident, was no longer nervous to read or write, and I felt like a new person. Two years later, at the end of seventh grade, I could finally tell you what a book was about after reading it. My writing improved; I actually enjoyed it. Everything finally started to make sense.

Although I was excelling academically to places I never thought I could reach, my friends in public school still could not recognize that I actually had problems with learning. They thought it was funny to call me "retarded" and single me out as someone who went to a school for kids with special needs. Again, I went along with their jokes because at the time, my friends were all I had.

At the beginning of my eighth-grade year, I could finally read and write like everyone else, so I wanted to return to public school. It seemed like my public school friends were all having fun. Socially, I was miserable. I also felt I was no longer being challenged academically. For these reasons, I was ready to move on.

The administration at AIM Academy encouraged me to stay. Even though I had learned to read and write, they assured me I could still benefit greatly from the unique education they offered. One teacher in particular, Mr. Chris Herman, assured me that by using AIM's connections and resources, I could build a network that would enable me to become an entrepreneur. AIM offered to give me a tour of their high school. I agreed to check it out.

I was instantly captivated by a program called Schoolyard Ventures, which helps high school students in the Philadelphia area start their own businesses. The program provides loans, mentors, and all the resources necessary to start a business. On the tour, representatives from this program asked if I had any business ideas. How could I expand a project or company? How could I market it? I didn't know the answers to half of these questions, and this was a tipping point for me. I was actually being challenged. That tour made me realize there were some incredible educational opportunities beyond just reading, writing, and math. If I stayed at AIM, I could actually start my own business.

Newly energized, I told Mr. Herman I would stay enrolled as long as I could participate in this high school entrepreneurship program as an eighth grader. He laughed, amused that I was already starting to counteroffer when I wasn't even in the program yet. But AIM accepted my offer, so I stayed and started working with Schoolyard Ventures to launch my own companies.

Schoolyard Ventures began as a nonprofit called Startup Corps, with the sole purpose of helping high school students start businesses. Startup Corps eventually licensed out their curriculum and became Schoolyard Ventures, which is a for-profit enterprise. The program's instructors were not AIM Academy employees. Instead, they were outside professional entrepreneurs who came in to teach for a couple of hours, twice a week. They questioned and challenged us about how we should price products, market them, and keep track of finances. They challenged us to execute, and were there to help if we ran into problems.

Initially, I launched several small, simple businesses. For example, I went around to family and friends with iPhones and charged them a small fee to replace their damaged screens. I would also camp outside shoe stores the night before they released a new set of exclusive Nike sneakers. I would scoop up several pairs of shoes, then resell them online or at conventions for up to four times what I paid for them. I bought shoes for $175 and sold them for $1,500.

I enjoyed making thousands of dollars at these small-time endeavors. Before long, though, I wanted to create something original. In the beginning, I had been hustling mostly just to make money. Now, I was feeling challenged to do something more meaningful.

As Chris Burch, cofounder of Tory Burch and CEO of Burch Creative Capital, told me in an interview, "The biggest mistake millennials are making is that they are starting companies (products or services) that only *they* individually need. There are so many other opportunities they should explore." Taking this to heart, I asked myself, "What is a potential problem I might help solve through my entrepreneurship?" Soon, I hit upon an answer.

I realized I was getting an amazing education at AIM, but I also realized it was costing tens of thousands of dollars per year. The maximum scholarship my school was able to provide was up to 50 percent of the tuition. I thought there had to be a solution to this problem, and that inspired the idea for my first original business. I teamed up with my best friend Sophia Gross, who also goes to AIM, to launch an organization called Opportunity Rise.

We started out by producing clothing apparel and branding it with our logo, promoting the message that everyone has the opportunity to rise. We gave 50 percent of our revenue to scholarship funding at AIM Academy. The rest went toward expenses like travel for speaking engagements to promote the business. Our goal was to sell our apparel and successfully brand it in order to raise awareness and money for kids with learning disabilities like us.

Soon, the business began to take off. The coolest part was seeing kids from all around the area wearing our apparel with our logo. Whenever someone asked them what the logo on their shirt meant, the awareness could spread. Our initial success led to an opportunity to present a TEDx Talk in which Sophia and I discussed how to turn a difficulty into a success.

We were spreading our message about turning an apparent disadvantage into a competitive advantage. We got a lot of traction from that presentation. It did not go viral. We did not get a million views. However, I used my entrepreneurial mind-set to market it. I sent the video of our presentation to other TED Talk speakers, pointing out how our concept was similar to theirs.

Before long, responses came back. The first was from Angela Lee Duckworth, PhD, a professor at University of Pennsylvania. Duckworth is a specialist in the psychological traits of grit and self-control.

Duckworth's TED Talk is titled "The Key to Success? Grit." Our TED Talk is titled "Difficulty to Success." But when you type "Difficulty to Success TED Talk" into Google, Duckworth's presentation pops up first (no surprise there because hers has more than 8.5 million views). I sent her an e-mail, jokingly expressing my frustration about the confusion between our Ted Talk titles. She responded that she loved my enthusiasm and invited me to speak at The Character Lab, her nonprofit workshop advancing the science and practice of character development at the University of Pennsylvania.

At her lab, I discussed how people with learning disabilities are often "grittier" than others. Duckworth's research has been highly influential to my own self-awareness about when to quit and when to press on in pursuit of a goal, and I was honored to be the youngest person to ever speak at her lab.

Encouraged by Duckworth's response, I started e-mailing other influential, successful people in the Philadelphia area. I got a response from Daniel Fine, who has since become an integral part of my life and has helped me greatly in countless ways.

Daniel is three people to me: a boss, a brother, and an inspiration. Sometimes he's all three in a day. As my boss, he gives me instructions on how to best do my job. As a brother, he may tackle me on a couch and give advice on life. As an inspiration, he shows me what is possible when you have an entrepreneurial spirit and work hard.

I first met Daniel when he was a junior at the University of Pennsylvania. We were both working in the same office space, an inner-city building filled with bright colors, chalkboards, and inspirational quotes. Schoolyard Ventures rented out the space for high school students to work on their fledgling businesses after school. At the time, Daniel was using the space as an office for his company Glass-U, which makes unique, customizable sunglasses. Glass-U has licensing agreements with many major universities, fraternities, and sororities. They also have exclusive rights to make sunglasses for the FIFA World Cup.

One day after school, I was in the office doing some work for Opportunity Rise. Normally, the environment was pretty quiet. Suddenly, I heard a loud shout nearby. I left my desk to check it out. It was Daniel, excited that *Huffington Post* founder Arianna Huffington had just posted a photo of herself wearing a pair of his company's shades. I congratulated him. Daniel asked how my company was doing. We hit it off, and he offered me an internship at Glass-U.

I jumped at the chance. It was summer 2014. At fourteen years old, I was the youngest person in the company; the oldest was twenty-three. As an intern, I started out selling sunglasses at street festivals, then worked my way up to trade shows.

I still work for Glass-U. Now I manage some sales and marketing, as well as business-to-business (B2B) promotional and retail sales. I help them to effectively market our product using social media. In recent years, I have also started to help find investors. Today, Glass-U is fortunate to enjoy the support of many influential investors who have trusted and believed in us. I've enjoyed watching the business grow, and I'll always be grateful to Daniel for giving me the opportunity to be a part of it.

Working at Glass-U and Opportunity Rise boosted my confidence. I was growing more motivated to become the next great entrepreneur. I soon realized, though, there were hundreds of kids like me, and these were the people I needed to be associating with. So I started joining groups of young entrepreneurs on Facebook. It was awesome to develop new friendships with kids who shared the same passions I did. We would go to lunches, conferences, and other events where we could hear inspirational speakers like entrepreneurs Peter Thiel and Mark Cuban. My circle was expanding, and I enjoyed getting inspired.

For the next year, I kept busy. I went to school from 8:00 a.m. to 3:00 p.m. every day. I played sports after school, had dinner with my family, and then did homework. I hung out with Sophia, many nights until 3:00 a.m., creating shirt designs and presentations for Opportunity Rise. I also continued as an intern at Glass-U, mostly working remotely and coming into the office when I had free time.

In 2015, I wanted to try something new, so I went to live in London for the summer. I interned for a company called The Beans Group, which is a parent company to multiple youth-oriented businesses. I worked for two of their child companies. The first, Student Beans, sells software to companies for their online shops, verifying if someone is a student at checkout. The second company, Voxburner, focuses exclusively on marketing to youth and hosts two annual events that attract thousands of marketing executives from various companies.

Inspired by this experience, I returned to the United States with a new passion for marketing to the millennial generation. I was starting to realize how powerful we can be as both workers and consumers. How could we best utilize that untapped power? How could I help brands connect better with our generation?

I was also struck by the growing awareness that in the past few years, I had accomplished more than I'd ever imagined I could, despite my learning disabilities. It is so easy to think that a learning disability will prevent you from being successful. I was more determined than ever to end that misperception.

People with learning disabilities tend to lack strengths from the right side of their brain, which is responsible for reading, writing, and comprehension. They have more qualities of the left side, which favors the arts and sciences. Entrepreneurship is a left-brain trait. As I researched this phenomenon, I learned that some of the top entrepreneurs, actors, and scientists—people I look up to—also had learning disabilities. Among them are Oprah Winfrey, Richard Branson, and Steve Jobs. Despite disabilities, including dyslexia, all have been very successful.

In my experience, having a learning disability is no match for having a passion. Many people are successful because they simply found their passion and developed a plan to put it into action. Fashion designer Daymond John is a great example. He had a passion for designing clothes and then used the left side of his brain to create Fubu, one of the top-selling fashion brands of the past two decades.

Like Daymond John, millennials have the ability to find their passion early on and combine it with their strengths. For example, are you passionate about coffee and coding? Then combine the two: code a website and talk all about coffee. It doesn't matter what it is. If you combine your passion with something you're good at, there is a lot of room to become successful.

Millennials need to bet on their strengths, not their weaknesses. I do not regret the time I spent working so hard to learn to read and write. It changed my life. But what if I had spent more time improving what I was already good at? For example, I was one grade level below the norm in reading. As a result, I focused more on improving my reading. But maybe I should have been focusing harder on public speaking—my strength—because it was eventually going to help me with my future. Maybe I should have focused harder on learning how to market products rather than how to read Shakespeare.

I have been able to find success at a young age by focusing on my passions and my strengths. All millennials can do the same, and we can help improve the world in the process. So, how do you define *millennial*?

Millennials are _____.

Millennials are _____.

Millennials are _____.

Give me a few chapters, and I'll help fill in the blanks.

CHAPTER 1

THE PLUGGED-IN GENERATION

MILLENNIALS ARE the first generation who grew up surrounded by technology, computers, and more recently, social media. We've never known any other way of life. We can be interactive with all these different resources. We can get in touch with as many people as we want. We can learn for free. We can do all this from a very young age.

Before the age of two, my little cousin Misha was already tech savvy. Before he had a full vocabulary or could even read or build blocks, he could play Angry Birds on Facebook. He could even make a FaceTime call on an iPhone. As they grow up, many millennials are using their technological expertise to impact culture and society.

Consider Kelvin Doe, a teenager from Sierra Leone. At the age of thirteen, Doe taught himself engineering. Using discarded scrap metals, he constructed transmitters, generators, and batteries. He eventually created his own radio station, broadcasting music and news under the name DJ Focus. Doe's mother initially thought he was just playing with trash, but he proved how productive a millennial can

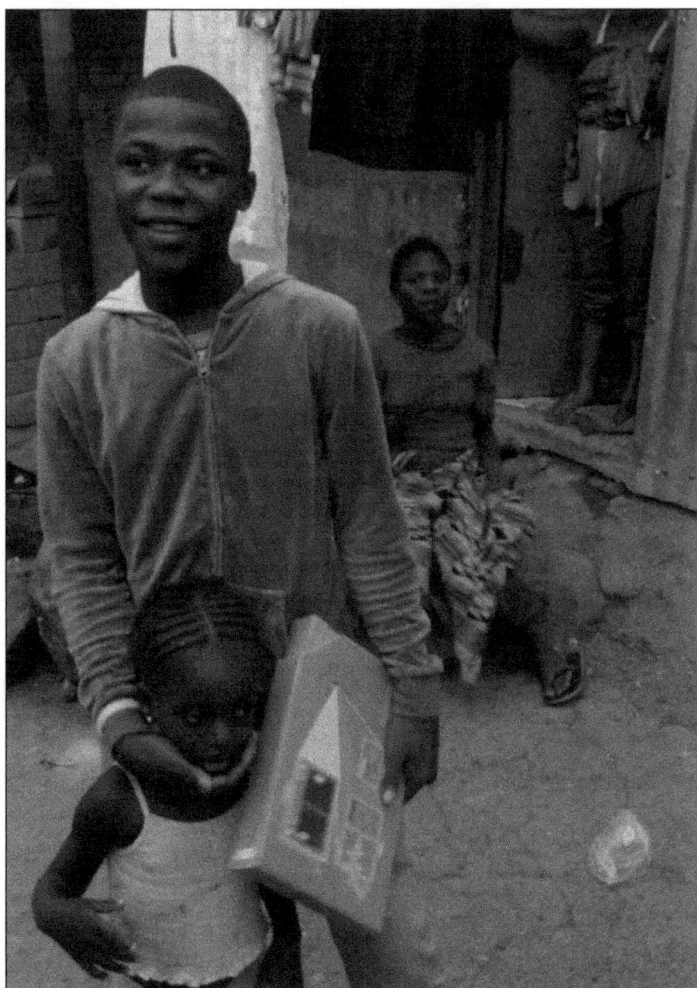

be by combining personal passion with access to technology. After attracting international attention for his work, the resourceful tech prodigy became the youngest person to participate in MIT's Visiting Practitioner's Program.

As mentioned earlier, many people wrongly believe that millennials primarily use social media for frivolous purposes, like posting photos of themselves getting drunk at parties. But the reality is that, like Kelvin Doe, most millennials are using social media much more productively. They are using it to brand themselves, find job opportunities, gain knowledge, share information, and connect with people.

For example, I'm Facebook friends with some of the top CEOs from around the world. I simply friended them, chatted, and now we are connected. These are multimillionaire entrepreneurs who have started hugely successful companies that I have been able to connect with by using social media in a productive way.

The power of connectivity cannot be overstated. Millennials have unprecedented access to other people. It has never been easier to get in contact with someone. You just have to be smart about it. I have gotten in contact with some of the top entrepreneurs from around the world. I did not e-mail them endless paragraphs about why I wanted to talk to them. I e-mailed them a short-and-sweet message, and then asked for ten to fifteen minutes of their time the following week to talk. It usually works.

This would simply not have been possible in the past. What

did it mean to be connected thirty years ago? In the late 1980s, people were just discovering e-mail. Cell phone use was not yet widespread. There was no such thing as social media as we know it today. Millennials are more connected than any other generation. This gives us advantages that previous generations did not enjoy. In addition to being able to connect more easily, we also have the power to promote ourselves, whether it be to a future employer or a potential romantic interest.

I probably watch two hours of television a week. This is not because I don't enjoy it, but I'd rather spend time using social media as a means of connecting with people and learning. For me, that's more entertaining than watching a TV show. Even better, it's a form of *productive entertainment*. By reading online articles the night before, I go into my next day with stronger knowledge.

Millennials are intuitive about accessing information. It comes naturally because we've been plugged in from birth, as opposed to previous generations who had to go to a library to find information. Today, if we need to find out who America's twenty-second president was (Grover Cleveland), we can just go on Google. This is not because we are lazy or incapable of finding the answer in some other way. It's because we put a high value on time and convenience.

We are a fast-paced generation, and time is precious to us. Why would we spend time digging up a book in a library when we have access to Google at our fingertips? I honestly believe I can learn more in an hour on social media by reading articles, stories, current events, and history than I might by sitting in a classroom for the same amount of time.

One of my favorite sources of information is Snapchat, an app that allows you to send a brief photo, video, or text, which gets deleted after one to ten seconds. Snapchat has a feature called Discover on which media outlets (ESPN, CNN, BuzzFeed, and others) are constantly posting content and informational tips, all geared toward millennials. The Discover feature allows you to preview this content for a few seconds and then decide if you want to read further or move on.

This is a very practical tool for getting information. After all, why do I need to watch an entire episode of a news program just to learn that a bank was robbed? Instead, I can just look at my phone. I can read the headline on Snapchat, scroll down my Facebook news feed, or read 140 characters on Twitter. Millennials are a "headline generation." Technology enables us to become informed in a more economical, fast-paced way. Again, it provides productive, rather than passive, entertainment.

In addition to Snapchat, we enjoy access to websites like BuzzFeed and Elite Daily, unique online magazines that provide fun, interactive ways to access information. These sites know that our generation is not always going to grab the *New York Times* or *Wall Street Journal* and read a ten-minute article. We would rather check out BuzzFeed, which has a three-minute article with interactive games, lists, and personal quizzes on topics we relate to.

We are not a *New York Times* generation. We don't want to read a Sunday paper. We prefer Buzzfeed and similar media outlets because they allow us to maximize our time, and they relate to us on a more personal level.

Please don't misunderstand; I'm not saying we want information dumbed down for us. We still want facts from reliable sources. We just want to access them in a simpler, faster way. We want to be able to click on a news feed, quickly read an article, and then tell our friends what we learned the next day. Our generation is connected to one another all the time, and we benefit from one another's knowledge.

Social media also gives us the ability to surround ourselves with people who have similar passions, interests, and goals. Facebook and Instagram are great examples. People are not friending one another online just because they're already friends in person. They are friending one another because they've met someone who shares a passion for travel or specialized foods. They're connecting on social media based on their similar interests. They're gaining knowledge from one another, whether it's sharing a news article about a topic they enjoy, or posting a photo of a shared favorite spot while traveling abroad.

It's all about finding your passion and sharing it. As offensive as it sounds, Mark Zuckerberg and his college roommates had a passion for rating girls, which led them to create a website called Hot or Not. This site eventually became Facebook, one of the largest and most influential companies in the world. Finding your passion and then using your resources to act upon that passion are the keys to becoming successful in the millennial generation.

One of the most important ways to do this is by effectively branding yourself. This is not limited to just people who want to create a personal brand. You could be a high school athlete, a ballerina, or an actor. Whoever you are, under-standing how to package and promote yourself is a vital skill. You just have to find your strength and from there, build your brand. Social media allows you to do that more than ever.

Consider a young woman named Andini Makosinski. She

was interested in science, specifically in how the sun works. Andini created the first solar-powered flashlight. She brought it to a science fair and used social media to package, brand, and market it to her friends and family. Eventually, TV host Jimmy Fallon interviewed her about her product, and she was selling thousands of her flashlights.

Another example of successful self-branding is my friend Reece Whitley. He is a six-foot-nine high school swimmer. Reece grew up in my neighborhood. He goes to the William Penn Charter School in Philadelphia. Reece is one of the top swimmers in the United States and qualified for the Olympic Trials. He continues to break records and tie swim times set by Olympic champion Michael Phelps.

Reece is using his brand to help others. He plans on hosting clinics at pools across Philadelphia where kids can learn the sport of swimming. "The possibilities are endless in terms of what I can do to reach out to inner-city kids and spread the sport of swimming," Reece told me. His advice is the same as mine: always start by finding your passion.

"Experimenting and searching is the hardest part of realizing what it is that you love. Whether it's a sport or something else, you *must* be willing to search for the thing or things that make you happy," Reece said. "It may take you a long time to find what it is that you truly enjoy spending time on, but continuing to look is more beneficial than simply giving up. If you find that it is a sport you love, roll with it and work at it as long as you can or until it does not become fun anymore. Once the fun is taken out of something that you invest your valuable time into, it no longer becomes healthy for you to do."

Reece has found his passion. He is using his resources to help others, and to connect with the right coaches and compete at the right events. In 2015, Reece was named *Sports Illustrated Kids'* SportsKid of the Year. To win that honor, he had to receive the most votes of all the nominees. He posted consistently on social media. He promoted his brand. That's something a previous generation was simply not able to do.

Another example is Stacey Ferreira, someone I have known for a few years now. In high school, Stacey took computer programming classes and learned how to code. After graduating, she gained acceptance to New York University and planned to start attending in the fall. Before school started, though, she spent the summer in Los Angeles with her brother Scott.

Together, they started a company called My Social Cloud. Like a few other companies, it keeps track of passwords to all of a user's different websites. For example, when you go to Facebook, it will automatically log in for you, in case you forgot your password. Even if your computer crashes, your secure passwords are always saved on your My Social Cloud account.

One day, Stacey saw that billionaire entrepreneur Sir Richard Branson had tweeted an announcement about an upcoming one-day charity event in Miami, Florida. The event offered the chance to meet Branson, but the entry fee was $2,000. Stacey called her dad and asked for a loan so she and her brother could fly to Miami to meet the famous entrepreneur. She promised to pay her father back. Within twenty-four hours, she and her brother were in Miami meeting Branson.

One week later, Branson and his team invested in Stacey's business. My Social Cloud was not particularly unique. There were other companies like it. However, Branson was impressed by Stacey's vision and determination to fly out and meet him, and that's why he invested. And it all started when she saw a simple tweet.

Thanks to social media, Stacey gained access to a celebrity who would have been almost entirely unreachable to a previous generation. Less than a year after Branson invested, Stacey had an exit strategy for her company. Not even twenty years old, she is now a multimillionaire in the process of launching a new business.

Andini Makosinski, Reece Whitley, and Stacey Ferreira are just a few examples of millennials using technology to pursue their dreams and positively impact the world. I believe there are countless other success stories waiting to happen. We live in an exciting age where being plugged in allows us the potential to partner with some of the smartest and brightest people in the world. By connecting with the right people and combining our passions with our strengths, there are fewer limits than ever to what we might accomplish.

CHAPTER 2

WHAT MILLENNIALS HAVE TO OFFER

WE OFTEN HEAR that many of the qualities that distinguish millennials will also end up hurting them in the workforce. On the contrary, these qualities are actually strengths. Employers who understand this will reap the benefits.

One of my greatest strengths is reaching out to people, cold e-mailing, and networking. Not long ago, I asked my mentor, business coach Cameron Herold, if he would introduce me via e-mail to his friend Simon Sinek. Simon promotes the concept of starting with "why" and not "how" or "what" in the field of marketing. His TED Talk on this topic is the third most viewed in the world. Starting with "why" totally shifts the way the mind works in terms of marketing and presenting yourself. Simon consults with companies to help them utilize this concept to their advantage.

I thought Simon might relate to my idea of how learning disabilities are an advantage instead of a disadvantage. Cameron agreed to make the introduction and sent Simon an e-mail. Unfortunately, there was no response.

A month later, it occurred to me that I still had Simon's e-mail address because I had been CC'd on Cameron's message to him. I decided to cold e-mail Simon and introduce myself, mentioning that I was referred by his friend

Cameron Herold. Once again, no response. A few days later, though, I got a call from a private number: "Hello, Andrew. This is Simon Sinek."

I was stunned. I really didn't know what to say. Here I was talking to a guy who has over twenty-five million views on a TED Talk. We had a normal conversation for about twenty minutes. We talked about his idea of starting with "why," and he shared his thoughts about the concept of kids with learning disabilities having an advantage.

To me, that was a great example of what can happen when you continue to try and refuse to accept "no" for an answer. Cameron Herold's initial e-mail introduction didn't get a response, but I refused to give up. I e-mailed Simon personally and eventually got the reward of a phone call from him. Since that call, Simon has set me up with his consulting team, and they've been helping me find my "why."

Millennials often get a bad rap from Generation Y and baby boomers. We are often perceived as distracted, lazy, and irresponsible. These are misperceptions. Like any other generation, we are willing to work hard when we find something we are passionate about. Companies could benefit by tapping into the work ethic that comes from that passion. As it is, not enough companies are currently placing bets on millennials.

Consider a company like Chipotle. A large part of their target market is young people who want to enjoy a cheap, quick Mexican meal. Why aren't companies like Chipotle hiring millennials to help with their marketing? Instead, they're hiring people who have a wealth of experience in traditional marketing to brand their company to a generation that has a totally different sense of the market. Companies need to start benefiting from millennials to help reach that target market.

What sorts of benefits do millennials offer? For one, millennials are community-minded, and therefore, we are great at teamwork. As an example, let's look at Facebook again. Most people know the story. It started in a Harvard dorm room and grew at a rapid pace. After attracting some of the top investors in Silicon Valley, the company relocated to the West Coast.

Once they opened their 430,000-square-foot headquarters in Menlo Park, founder Mark Zuckerberg made it very clear that he's a millennial running a company that is widely used by millennials. Every day in their headquarters, thousands of millennials work to run the company, with Zuckerberg right in the middle of the activity, using the same-size desk and same computer as every other employee.

Companies like Facebook are demonstrating the community-minded power of recognizing everyone's value, having each employee work together and bounce ideas off one another. Whether it's an accountant, marketer, or graphic designer, Facebook focuses on each employee's strengths, encouraging them to collaborate as a community. This collaboration is something millennials do well.

Because of social media, millennials are also able to learn quickly and put that knowledge into action. Companies can benefit from millennials because we know how our generation learns and interacts. Previous generations mostly learned in a traditional way. They went to school, read textbooks, and watched news on TV. The millennial generation, however, is faster at learning anything they want, whenever they want. With abundant technology at our disposal, it's easier than ever to learn. Whether it's YouTube, Facebook, or other social media platforms, the power to learn is literally right at our fingertips.

I believe that millennials' brains have come to be wired differently than those of previous generations. We have been wired in such a way that time is of the essence. Information arrives and is absorbed faster. For instance, when 9/11 happened, many people didn't hear about it until a few hours later. Even just fifteen years ago, the technology was not that fast. Today, being able to absorb information faster allows our brains to operate at a higher speed.

Once again, Snapchat is an example. Young entrepreneur Evan Spiegel picked up on the fact that some people were tired of simply texting. People wanted the visual experience of actually seeing someone, in addition to reading text. As a result, Evan created Snapchat, which exploded in popularity. In 2016, Snapchat hit eight billion daily video views.

Does the amount of time millennials spend connected slow us down when it comes to getting work done? No. On the contrary, it makes us better at multitasking.

For example, some people complain about young people using their cell phones at the dinner table. Of course, this is a sign of disrespect and bad manners. People should know the appropriate time to use technology. But overall, I believe the millennial generation has learned to know when being connected through technology is inappropriate and when it's actually a benefit.

It may not seem like it, but most of the time, we are going online only to learn, connect with someone, or participate in a like-minded community. This is not necessarily interrupting our current task. It is enabling us to perform more than one task. That is a valuable skill in the workplace.

Other generations wonder why we're never looking up from our phones or computers. They think we're just playing games or sending naked pictures. On the contrary, we're using technology to learn and connect. Again, it's a form of productive entertainment.

Another strength of millennials is that we are constantly active. The average college student spends fifteen hours a week in the classroom. Add homework and other learning outside the classroom, and that number doubles. Young people are away from home for the first time, without their parents telling them when to eat and go to sleep. They may have a class at eight o'clock in the morning, go back to their dorm, rest, do some work, get lunch with friends, go to a party, catch a nap, then wake up and do more work. They have to learn to manage their busy schedules, aware that even two wasted minutes could affect their entire day. Time is of the essence.

You could send a traditional text message in the same amount of time it takes to send a Snapchat video. But with Snapchat, you are able to see the emotion in a person's face, which adds to the quality of the communication. Whether it's silly, fun, or serious, every second matters in communication. Being able to communicate effectively in a fast-paced environment is very beneficial to companies.

Many companies are now starting to hire millennials, and these employers are growing more flexible with the traditional nine-to-five work mind-set. Another mentor of mine, Ben Kirshner, is the CEO of a company called Elite SEM, an agency that helps companies with search engine marketing. *Crain's* business magazine named Elite SEM as one of the top companies to work for in New York. Ben is doing what I believe all traditional companies should start doing: giving unlimited vacation time and not rigidly requiring employees to be in the office all the time.

"I don't believe in limiting people's time off," Ben told me. As a millennial, I really respect and love this concept. As long as I hit every deadline, attend every meeting, and take every call, there is no reason I should be limited to where and when I do my work.

This is not promoting selfishness or laziness. It is putting faith in employees. If you believe in them enough, they will get the work done. Google has put this into practice with great success. They offer unlimited vacation time and free lunch. As a result, employees realize they can save money on lunch and use that money in a better way. Google employees also have the option of doing yoga and exercise classes in the company's headquarters.

They are not being forced to sit at a desk all day. They can work in a community space with other people and work only the hours necessary to accomplish their tasks. They know they will get their work done better this way. However, their full potential may not be realized if they are forced to stick to a traditional nine-to-five mind-set, sit at a cubicle, have a one-hour lunch break, and get only two weeks of vacation.

A more flexible work environment benefits everyone. The company can see more productivity, and employees will be happier. Maybe an employee could schedule a trip to the Bahamas as long as s/he knows s/he has to get his/her work done that week. I believe in the next couple of years, we are going to start seeing many Fortune 500 companies switch to this model.

To sum up all these points, let's look at the Next Gen Summit, a movement started by Justin Lafazan, a twenty-year-old from New York who attends the University of Pennsylvania. Justin is an amazing entrepreneur who started his first company when he was thirteen.

Justin realized there were many entrepreneurial kids like himself, so with the help of a few friends, he started this movement that holds a summit once a year to discuss and promote entrepreneurship. The community also exists online. Currently, there are about one thousand members in Next Gen Summit's Facebook group.

Each member provides different values in a community filled with everyone from marketing specialists and MIT engineers, to graphic designers, computer scientists, and coders. Next Gen Summit is a great example of how the millennial generation uses technology to collaborate and get work done. It is a vast resource pool. Any member can ask any other member for help.

Questions come in all forms.

"Does anyone know a designer who can help me with this logo? I need this color scheme, and I need it in this format."

"Does anyone have a great computer engineer who can code an app for me? I'm willing to pay $10,000."

Whatever the request, all members are connected, forming a diverse group of people willing to help one another. Members hail from all over the United States, Asia, and many other places around the world, forming what we affectionately call the Next Gen "mafia."

This network has greatly helped me in my entrepreneurial career. I have been able to ask if anyone has advice on speaking to a group of CEOs about a particular topic. I have inquired if anyone has connections to certain top-level entrepreneurs.

All the members are just like me. We all share a passion for leadership and productivity. There are hundreds of millennials in this group. I have probably met only fifty of them in person, and yet I know I can message each and every one, and they will respond. That's how powerful it is when we're all willing and able to help one another, to collaborate and provide value to one another. As John F. Kennedy Jr. said, "A rising tide lifts all boats." Next Gen Summit empowers millennials to collaborate and benefit from one another in a way never possible to previous generations.

Next Gen Summit is a great example of the concepts we've talked about in this chapter—a community mindset, fast access to information, the ability to learn quickly, a connected environment, and the power of asking. Once companies realize they can take advantage of all these qualities in millennials, they'll see that what are often perceived as our weaknesses are, instead, great strengths.

CHAPTER 3

THE ENTREPRENEURIAL MINDSET

WHAT IS an entrepreneur? Is it a businessman with a briefcase, crunching numbers, making sales calls, and firing off e-mails? Maybe that's how people used to see it. In the past, entrepreneurship was not seen as "cool." To some people, being an entrepreneur meant you were terrible in school and had no idea what you were going to do with your life. As a result, you dropped out of high school or college, slept in your parents' basement, and maybe decided to start some enterprise as an escape route from real life.

Although that's maybe how people saw it thirty years ago, today that perception is changing. An entrepreneur can be anyone from an African-American woman born in Mississippi (Oprah Winfrey) to a young white Jewish kid in New York (Mark Zuckerberg). The millennial generation is filled with entrepreneurs, whether they know it or not. Whether it's someone running a nonprofit or someone blogging about raising kids, an entrepreneur is simply someone who identifies problems and then provides solutions to those problems. Sometimes that involves money; sometimes it doesn't.

Earlier, I mentioned Cameron Herold, my mentor and one of my biggest inspirations. Cameron is the former COO of 1-800-GOTJUNK, a company that clears out trash or old furniture for a small fee. Within seven years, Cameron took 1-800-GOTJUNK from a $2 million start-up to a $160 million company.

Today, Cameron is a coach for some of the world's most powerful CEOs. While preparing for my TEDx Talk, I was advised to watch as many talks as possible, and I kept coming back to Cameron's TEDx Talk. In it, he said that an entrepreneur is "someone who organizes, operates, and assumes the risk of a business venture."

This quote really struck me, and I decided to use it in our talk. Flash forward a few months. After our talk went live on YouTube, I decided to reach out to Cameron and tell him how much he had inspired me.

Three days later, I got an e-mail response. Cameron was encouraging but did not offer any assistance beyond some kind words. There was no need for me to respond, but I thought it was cool that such a successful entrepreneur had at least taken the time to encourage me. I soon forgot about our exchange.

A month later, while lying on the beach during my summer vacation, I got an unexpected phone call from the International Dyslexia Association (IDA). They told me they were honoring Cameron at their annual conference for his work inspiring young people with learning disabilities. I was stunned. I had personally admired Cameron, but up to that point, I was unaware he had a learning disability like me.

To my surprise, the IDA asked Sophia and me to introduce Cameron at that year's conference in San Diego. At the time, I had no idea that Cameron had personally chosen me and Sophia to introduce him. Apparently, he had heard of our work encouraging students with learning disabilities and thought we would be a perfect fit to introduce him.

On the trip to San Diego, I had a layover in Phoenix airport. There, I accidentally bumped into a guy, then quickly apologized and moved on. Later as the plane was about to take off, I got a tweet on my phone. It was from Cameron Herold. "Did you just bump into me in the airport?" he asked. I was amazed that this man who had been so influential to me—who had helped me rethink what it means to be an entrepreneur—was personally tweeting me.

At the IDA conference, I happily introduced Cameron before a crowd of two thousand people. I watched as he received the Pinnacle Award, an honor for those who inspire people with learning disabilities. Since then, Cameron has become an invaluable friend and mentor.

Cameron has taught me how to bring an entrepreneurial mind-set to all situations. To reiterate, he says an entrepreneur is someone who "organizes, operates, and assumes the risk" of a business venture. An entrepreneur doesn't just sit around hoping s/he is going to be successful. An entrepreneur organizes, operates, and honestly assumes the risk that if his/her venture doesn't work, s/he may not succeed. But it's a risk s/he's willing to take. As Chris Burch, CEO of Burch Creative Capital, says, "An entrepreneur is someone who is willing to take an enormous amount of risk, who is fearless, and avoids anything that is safe."

Being an entrepreneur also means being able to execute. You may e-mail fifty people in a day, ask for their help, try to sell them a product, or try to get them to use your service. It's knocking on doors. Entrepreneur Mark Cuban says he absolutely loves the people who go out and knock on doors to sell their product.

When Cameron was about seven years old, he identified a problem: every time he removed his shirt, he noticed that the coat hanger was just being thrown out. He realized that local dry cleaners were buying coat hangers at the time. So he went down to his basement where his mom saved all his coat hangers, took them to the dry cleaner, and sold them for a few cents each.

After realizing he could sell his old coat hangers to the dry cleaner, he went knocking on doors asking neighbors if he could have their unused coat hangers. They thought he was just some weird little kid with a coat hanger fetish, but he didn't care. He *organized* his supplies, *operated* by going out and knocking on doors, and *assumed the risk* that people might not help. But they did.

Again, these principles apply not only to people who want to start a business. Remember swimmer Reece Whitley? Every day, he assumes the risk that he could get injured or exhausted. Every day, he organizes. When he wakes up, he has two swim goal times written on the ceiling above his bed. First thing every morning, he's reminded that those are the two times he has to beat. That's the goal he needs to achieve to make it to the next Olympic Games.

Next, he operates. He lifts weights. He gets in the pool and trains. He also markets himself. He goes out and talks with people about his career. Reece is proof that being entrepreneurial is not necessarily starting a business. You can do it by being a swimmer. You can do it by being a basketball player, an actor, or a scientist. An entrepreneur is not just someone who makes money. Again, it's someone who finds a problem—whatever that may be—and provides a unique solution.

Where does this entrepreneurial mind-set come from? It often starts at a young age. As an example, let's look at another Cameron Herold story. In raising his children, Cameron doesn't take the traditional route that many parents do. Some parents make their children clean their room, wash the dishes, and take the dog for a walk, then at the end of the week, pay them $20 for their labors.

Instead, Cameron makes his kids walk around the house and pitch him on what chores have to be done, just like any other sales pitch. For example, his son will propose, "Dad, I want five dollars to pick all the weeds." Cameron will counter, "I'm going to pay you only three dollars." Cameron and his kids interact and bargain. This back-and-forth teaches them an entrepreneurial mind-set early on.

It also teaches the value of identifying problems and taking initiative. A kid can realize that weeds need to be picked or tiles need to be scrubbed. They realize the value of these activities for the house and the family, as well as the monetary value they'll receive for their time and effort.

This entrepreneurial parenting style also benefits the parents, of course. Many parents may not have the time, energy, or money to get all the household chores done on a regular basis. Using Cameron's method, however, parents enjoy a cost-efficient means of maintaining the household while their children learn the value of hard work, how to take initiative, and pitch ideas. Everybody wins.

Using this creative method, parents can greatly impact how their child's brain develops. This also goes for the kinds of bedtime stories parents tell their children. When I was growing up, the stories my parents shared were not just "happily ever after" fairy tales where something good always happens to the characters in the end. Kids can learn from stories where things don't always go well, and the characters have to figure a way out of their problems and learn from their failures. This is true for the stories you hear before bed, the TV shows you watch, and the games and sports you play.

I don't remember the last time I played video games. That's not just because I would rather go to networking events or hear an inspirational speaker. I try to be aware of the value of my time. If I'm playing video games 24-7, I'm less likely to go out and find value in other real-world situations. Personally, I feel there's much more value in playing an actual game of basketball than in playing Madden for an hour. This is true from both a physical health standpoint and a problem-solving standpoint.

Some gamers would argue that you can learn problem-solving skills from video games, too. There's some truth to this.

However, nothing beats the actual experience of playing in real life.

Personally, playing basketball for an hour helps me with problem solving. I can apply those problem-solving skills to other areas of life. I can compare a pick and roll to getting a seed round of funding for a start-up company. Once I get past that pick and roll, I can drive to the basket; once I get that seed round of funding, I can go out and start making prototypes of my product. Then I make the shot; I have the prototype and I can start selling. Then I make the basket. These lessons are going to help me win the game—on the court and in business.

Lewis Howes, author of *New York Times* bestseller *The School of Greatness*, affirms the importance of sports in building confidence and skills. A dyslexic like me, Howes told me, "I felt dumb all the way through college. School was very challenging, and this made me very insecure. Sports was my outlet to build confidence and learn how to connect ideas into action."

Not only is a game like basketball fun to play, but it also teaches you to work with others. It helps you identify their strengths and how they can best contribute to the team. If you're an employer, it can help you identify which employee might have the skill to create a strong marketing campaign.

It can teach you to identify the unique value that each person brings.

If someone is going to play a team sport, s/he is going to have to work with people. S/he is going to have to understand people's different strengths and weaknesses, just like s/he would have to know an employee's strengths and weaknesses when running a business or other enterprise. It teaches collaboration.

Growing up, I always wanted to try tennis. Tennis is not a bad sport, but it's a sport you do on your own, without the help of a whole team. For the most part, my parents did not allow me to play those kinds of single-player sports. They only allowed me to play basketball in the winter, baseball in the spring, and whatever sport I chose in the fall. My parents wanted me to be part of a team, whether it was a sport or a club like the Boy Scouts, where I had to work with a diverse group of kids.

Early on, I was resentful of this, but I thank them for it now. I see the value in it. I'm not saying you should not play tennis, golf, or any other individual sport. But when I was growing, I believe playing team sports really helped foster the entrepreneurial mind-set that has made me who I am today.

I believe parents should raise their children to not simply go to school and become a doctor or lawyer but to be entrepreneurs in whatever form that takes. Unlike thirty years ago, entrepreneurship is sexy now. It's cool. The entrepreneurial mind-set is important for every millennial, whether they choose to be an athlete, an entertainer, a marketer, or anything else.

As I have learned, it helps to start young in developing an entrepreneurial mind-set. Regardless of when you start, though, the key is to focus on identifying and solving problems you see around you. One crucial way you can start to consciously develop this mind-set is by being aware of the people with whom you surround yourself.

CHAPTER 4

FINDING YOUR CIRCLE

SCHOOLS OFTEN TEACH you to avoid bad influences. The most successful people, however, go beyond this. They want everyone in their life to be a *good* influence—someone who inspires them to succeed.

It is important to surround yourself with people who have the same passion and enjoy doing the same activities as you, whether it is selling a product or playing a sport. It is important to understand how each person can provide value to your life, and how you can provide value to theirs. I try my best to do that.

I have different groups of friends. Some are friends from school, others from outside school, and some I have met from traveling. I know that each of them provides me value, and I do the same for them, whether on a large or small scale. What do I mean by value? It's simply helping one another any way we can, whether it's giving advice or providing a place to stay while traveling.

I also enjoy being part of a network of people in their twenties, thirties, and forties. Even as a high school student, I've been able to surround myself with people who are in college, those who have dropped out, and everything in between. Age does not matter. We can all still learn from and help one another.

Earlier, I mentioned a company I work for called Glass-U. The company is staffed exclusively with millennials. (Yes, I know it's a scary thought to some, but it is the future, and we have been very successful so far.) Despite the slight age difference among some of the employees, we are connected by our shared interest of growing the company. We each take our passions and our strengths (finance, marketing, design, etc.) and apply them toward that shared goal.

Finding your circle does not mean you have to share the exact particular interests as other people. You just want to find people who are as passionate about what they love as you are about what you love.

One of my best friends, Austin, is an actor who will be attending an arts school when he graduates high school. My friends Nathan and Will love entrepreneurship, like me. Will sells custom-made laser-engraved glass. Nathan creates custom tie-dyed surf fins, which he sells to the top retailers on the Jersey shore. Two other good friends, Michael and Joe, are both sports fanatics. They have an

encyclopedic knowledge of the Sixers, the Eagles, and other teams in the National Football League (NFL) and National Basketball Association (NBA). They use their knowledge to help other friends assemble the best fantasy sports teams.

Personality-wise, some of these guys are alike and some are different, but the common thread is that each of us has our own passions in life. We all benefit from one another's diverse knowledge and values, and we all have an entre-preneurial mind-set when approaching situations.

I have found that there are two ways to create a circle of people. The first way is to find friends who simply have a personality and interests similar to yours. For instance, you share the same taste in music, sports, and movies. The second way is to intentionally seek out people with shared

passions (entrepreneurship, acting, coding, etc.). I enjoy friends from both circles—some who are funny, love the same music, and play the same sports I play, and others who are driven entrepreneurs who love to work, work, work.

Stacey Ferreira is from the second circle, and she has been a big influence in my life. She started My Social Cloud, the password storage company I mentioned earlier. From an early age, Stacey knew the importance of surrounding herself with the right people. She knew it was going to be difficult to break into the tech community in Phoenix where she lived as a high schooler. So she moved to California and surrounded herself with similar-minded people.

In addition to positive friends, it is also crucial to find good mentors, people who have been where you want to go and can help you get there. My mentor, Cameron Herold, has helped with everything I touch in business. Cameron has lived the experience I am experiencing now: he struggled in school, was told he couldn't be successful due to his age and academic level, but he started businesses anyway. He's been there. I can relate to him on many different levels, mainly because he struggled just like I did.

Another mentor of mine is PJ Raduta. In the introduction, I mentioned Schoolyard Ventures, the high school entrepreneurship program hosted by AIM Academy. The program assigns each student a mentor to help him/her start his/her business. PJ was mine.

When I first had the idea for Opportunity Rise, I wanted people to see the logo on our sweatshirts and ask what it means. Whoever wore our shirts would be like walking billboards for the business, spreading our message about raising awareness for kids with learning disabilities.

At first, I planned to sell each sweatshirt for $15. Remember,

I was fourteen, this was my first original business, and I didn't know jack about pricing products, profit margins, or marketing. At the time, I was buying each sweatshirt for $10 (another mistake, but that is a different story).

My mentor, PJ Raduta, asked why I was pricing the shirts so low. He pointed out that if I walked into any college bookstore and bought a sweatshirt, I would be spending at least $60. This was for a shirt that cost less than $5 to make. Taking this lesson to heart, we started selling our Opportunity Rise sweatshirts for $30, making a solid profit margin of $20 on each unit sold. This was the first of many ways PJ opened my eyes to what was possible in business and marketing.

PJ provides so much value for me, and like every good relationship, I try to do the same in return, providing value for him in any way I can. For example, I have worked to help PJ and his team create the best possible academic curriculum for their students. As a student myself, I can bring a useful perspective to the process, one that provides a unique value for PJ and his students. I'm helping him like he has helped me.

At this point, you may be asking yourself how someone goes about finding great mentors. After all, most potential mentors don't give out advice and assistance for free. However, they do help those who provide value for them in return. Gary Vaynerchuk taught me this. Gary is an entrepreneur, public speaker, and author of several best-selling books. He was one of the first investors in Birchbox, Twitter, Medium, and other tech businesses. He bet on these companies early on, and his bets paid off.

Gary says the best way to create great relationships is by first providing value to someone multiple times. After you've done this, then you can ask for their help. He uses a boxing metaphor of "Jab, jab, jab, right hook" (also the title of his popular book). First, you jab (provide value to someone) several times, then you throw the right hook knockout punch (ask for value).

I have successfully followed this concept to create all kinds of productive relationships. By leveraging your strengths to provide value to people you admire, they will be much more willing to mentor and help you. There is a special lesson here for younger people: use your age to your advantage. Many successful entrepreneurs launched their first businesses at a young age, and they remember what it's like to struggle. This often makes them more willing to help younger people pursuing the same goals they had.

So why don't more people reach out to mentors in the way I describe? It's because many people are simply afraid of asking. In our generation, though, the power of technology makes it easier than ever to connect with people. We should not be afraid of using technology to ask people for help.

Don't be afraid to ask, and don't be afraid of the answer "no." The answer "no" should motivate you way more than the answer "yes" should. I fully believe that people who hear "no" more than "yes" are going to be more successful than those who always get whatever they want right away.

"No, I'm too busy to look at your project."

"No, I don't have time to take a meeting with you."

"No, we don't have enough room in our office to provide you an internship."

This is the kind of crap I have heard over and over again. Sure, you will inevitably have to accept some "nos" along the way. Still, keep trying. You are never going to get a "yes" unless you keep asking.

Ben Nemtin is the creator of the MTV show *The Buried Life*, a reality series where he and his friends attempted to complete a list of "100 things to do before you die." Ben says that the difference between people who are afraid to do awesome stuff and people who are actually doing it is about 99 percent to 1 percent. The reason the people actually doing amazing stuff are in the 1 percent is because the 99 percent were too afraid to try. Bottom line? If you are not afraid, your odds of success are much better.

Last year, I met Mark Cuban, and he said something that really made me think: "No balls, no babies." If you don't have the balls to go out and make it happen, there's never going to be any babies. This is true whether you're starting a business, trying to get an extension on a homework assignment, or even asking for a seat upgrade on a flight.

The power of asking means not being afraid. If you keep trying, accepting "no" sometimes as the answer but always striving for a "yes," I am confident you will eventually find success.

CHAPTER 5

SCHOOL IS NOT YOUR ENEMY

MANY PARENTS CONSTANTLY INSTILL in their children the importance of education. They warn their kids that they won't get anywhere in life unless they get As. For me, it was different.

I was fortunate that I was never pressured to just get As. My parents took another approach, simply encouraging me to do my best. It was not a passive approach. They taught me to prepare as much as I can, do all my homework, remember the information, and turn in every assignment on time.

However, my parents were always understanding if I didn't do well on a test or failed to provide enough information in a paper, resulting in a bad grade. As long as I put sufficient time into it, prepared, and did the best I could, they never really asked for more (so I guess this is that part where I say thanks for understanding, Mom and Dad).

As an entrepreneur in high school, my life is constantly busy and hectic. Does school get in the way of that? I used to think so.

When most students think about school, they think about getting their homework done and getting good grades. I see it differently. As an entrepreneur, I am constantly balancing meetings, phone calls, e-mails, and making my products the best they can be. That involves a lot of work. I can't just decide to put off an important e-mail until later in the day. I have to take ten to fifteen minutes to craft every e-mail. Ten or fifteen minutes is valuable time.

I will always choose a great opportunity, like speaking at an event or taking a meeting with a businessperson, over doing a homework assignment that's due the next day. I would rather get the late grade than hand it in on time and miss a potential career opportunity. I constantly ask myself what's going to help me more in the future: taking a meeting with the founder of a successful business, or turning in a paper comparing and contrasting two American presidents?

I'm not saying I never do homework and put all my time solely into business opportunities. School is very important to an extent, but there is no need to stress over it. If you are a student, learn as much as you can and get your work done, but also incorporate other opportunities into your school schedule.

School does not have to be the only route to success. It's not a matter of either/or: either school *or* some other opportunity. It's a matter of both/and: focus on school *and* other opportunities. Make time for and receive the benefits of both.

Don't be against school. Instead, learn to work *with* school. If you approach school the right way, it teaches you many good skills.

I approach my school work like I approach business. I have to make time to do market research. I have to carve out time to build a product. I have to test it. I have to review it and then bring in other advisers to hone it and improve on it. By relating my schoolwork to my passion for business, I have a more positive, productive mind-set. It may sound corny, but I really believe that.

The same mind-set would work for a musician. You have to find the right players for all the different parts of a song. You have to make sure each person individually has the right talents. You have to test them all together, and then you get the final product.

Working with school is the same. You see the bigger picture, the lessons it teaches you, and what value you can get out of it beyond just the quadratic formula or Modern Language Association (MLA) format. You have to understand how to relate it to your passions in real life.

Another important concept is this: Don't just think of homework as busy work. The concept of homework is not to tick off students and have them working around the clock. On the contrary, homework can teach you the valuable life skill of getting better through practice.

A classic question that comes up in math classrooms around the world is, "Why are we learning this because we will never use it in the real world?" I am not going to agree or disagree, but let me say this: whether you end up using certain math skills in the "real world," what you will benefit from is the value of practicing.

Why am I assigned forty trigonometry problems for homework when the test has only ten questions? It's so I can learn to keep practicing and consistently solving problems. That is a key skill to have in life and the workforce.

In school, you may be assigned a five-page essay to write after reading a book. Try not to look at this as drudgery. Try to see it from a different perspective. Rather than being a chore, doing this work is teaching you the value of repetition. Repetition is key to being able to fully understand a subject. I no longer see homework as busy work. I see it as a way to help me keep getting better at something every time I do it.

Last year, I took a class called Honors Art History, taught by an unbelievable AIM Academy instructor, Mr. Jesse Korff. It was one of my favorite classes. I both loved and hated it.

We never meet at a set time in a classroom. It was an online class where all the content was created and graded by Mr. Korff. The amount of work differed every week, but usually, it entailed reading around seventy pages of a textbook along with a few supplementary articles. Then we'd have to write a five-hundred-word summary or three-page essay about what we read. At one point, I got so far behind in the class that I had a 12.3 percent. Like I said, I loved the class. It was great.

Feeling frustrated, I said to Korff, "I am four weeks behind on my course work. I have more than four hundred pages to read. I have multiple essays to write. It will all be done for a late grade. But I would like to ask you something."

He looked at me with a blank stare. I continued. "Why?" I asked. "Why do you assign us so much work for an honors class that is technically an elective?" It just didn't make sense to me.

Korff gave me an answer I wasn't expecting. He said that I have a hard time with my brain's frontal lobe, which is responsible for memory. I am good at motivation, planning, and attention, but short-term memory tasks are a problem for me.

Korff said I was trying to do twenty-six hours' worth of work in twenty-four hours every day. I am a varsity basketball player, I go to school for nine hours, I run two companies, I have an internship, and I have to do homework. I also have to spend time with friends and family and occasionally even sleep. No wonder I was so far behind in the class.

Somehow, I managed to finish all the work and actually completed the class with an 86 percent. What that experience taught me is that school is not about getting overloaded with homework assignments. It is meant to teach you valuable lessons, and I don't mean lessons about cave paintings from 400 BCE. I mean lessons about how your brain works and the best way to buckle down and get work done.

It is not about testing your knowledge on a particular subject. It is about learning to manage your time and organize material. It is about teaching you valuable lessons you can use in the real world, no matter what job you have.

That experience taught me to understand my own learning style and how to maximize my time in order to better understand information. For example, if I'm assigned fifty pages of reading, I cannot spend the required time to do it. I cannot physically sit down and focus for that long. Of course, one reason for this is my dyslexia and ADHD.

In general, though, my learning style is different. I have to force myself to read and then go back and try to comprehend the material by reading chapter summaries, watching videos, and finding more background knowledge on the subject. I have to understand every aspect of the subject, and for me, this does not happen by reading alone.

School is not your enemy. You just need to see the bigger lessons it can teach you beyond simply absorbing the academic material and information. You have to figure out your own unique learning style and then put it into action.

As I mentioned earlier, the majority of real-life jobs are not going to require you to know about cave paintings. Unless you plan to become a professional historian, your job will probably never require you to know the exact date Japan bombed Pearl Harbor. However, skills like time management and writing are always valuable in the professional world, and school is a great place to build them. Good time management is the key to everything. As long as you can maximize your time and balance it with the right amount of effort, you are likely to be successful in whatever you do.

What if you are just not passionate about the material in a certain class? For example, I hate history. I never cared that a certain religion was founded in the BC era or a war started in 1918. Those facts are good to know, but they are not really going to help me in life or business.

To reiterate, millennials are a plugged-in generation who can access those kinds of facts almost instantly because of technology. But, in general, that information doesn't matter to us unless it somehow relates to our personal passion. I am not passionate about history, and try as you may, you'll never get me to like it.

So how do I motivate myself to tackle material I dislike? I shift my perspective and see it through a different lens. For example, during World War II, President Harry Truman had to weigh the cost/benefit of dropping the nuclear bomb on Japan. If he dropped it, X amount of people would die, and a certain amount of land would be polluted and destroyed. On the other hand, many American soldiers would be saved.

I could relate this dilemma to my own entrepreneurial mind-set. What will happen if we launch a certain marketing campaign? How many people might be offended by a certain approach, and how many people are we going to reach? Learning becomes easier when I am able to relate it to my own passion. This may not be as easy with subjects like math or reading, but the point is to try to relate what you are learning to your personal passion.

In school, I see myself as a "student entrepreneur." I have to finish all my homework and complete every assignment to the best of my ability. So what is the general message when it comes to school? You have a lot of control over how you approach it. School can be a training ground for bigger opportunities.

Going to school should not just be about getting good grades; it should be to learn skills that will help you become successful in all areas of life. If you want to develop an entrepreneurial mind-set, think of school as your training ground. That is much better than wasting energy resenting it.

CHAPTER 6

MAKING THE CONNECTION

SO FAR THROUGHOUT THIS BOOK, I have mostly been speaking as a millennial to other millennials. I have talked about our passion and potential as a uniquely plugged-in generation. In this chapter, I'd like to shift the conversation a little to address employers and brands that have a product or service geared toward millennials.

How can future employers best take advantage of our strengths and skills? In addition to the value we can provide, millennials are also a powerful group of consumers. We love to shop. So how can companies enable us to connect better with their brands? In this chapter, we'll consider these questions, as well as look at some companies that are successfully connecting with millennials.

For our generation, nothing is more important than authenticity. Millennials are the "BS detector" generation. We are able to tell when something is inauthentic or too good to be true. Therefore, brands should be honest in their advertising.

In the 2003 movie *Elf*, Will Ferrell's naïve character leaves the North Pole for the first time and visits New York City. He goes nuts when he sees a restaurant sign advertising the "World's Best Cup of Coffee." He actually believes the claim and can't wait to try it. It's a cute moment, but it points to a larger issue about truth in advertising. Outrageous claims might work on Buddy the Elf, but millennials are a bit more skeptical. We are jaded but in a healthy way. We value authenticity because it is rare.

Until recently, companies trying to reach our generation have used very traditional marketing, such as "Buy one, get one 50 percent off" signs on billboards and buses. Some companies send out e-mail blasts or snail-mail ads. This isn't going to fly with millennials. In fact, some of the companies that connect best with our generation are ones that never even offer discounts (we'll get into that shortly).

In order to come across as authentic, a company must understand every aspect of their target market. For example, where are their customers from? Are they mainly from the Midwest or the East Coast? What kind of music do they listen to? Which actors and movies do they love and follow? How are they communicating with their friends?

I cannot emphasize this enough: every single aspect of our lives is important to understand if you want us to connect with your brand. And it all starts with content. More companies need to realize that if they pump out relatable content as quickly as any other media outlet, they are much more likely to keep us as customers. What's more, if they hook us with relatable content, we will retweet, like, comment, and share their brand with our network of friends and family.

Millennials do not always prefer advertisements with the most high-definition image or the best photoshopped picture. Millennials appreciate when companies use "real" people to market a product or service. A model posing for a swimsuit line does not have to be the woman every guy dreams of or who every woman wants to be.

As an example, *Sports Illustrated* recently featured model Robyn Lawley in its famous swimsuit issue. Lawley was the first plus-size model to appear on the cover. Many women find Lawley to be more realistic and relatable, which makes them more likely to buy the swimsuit she's wearing. They can more easily imagine themselves in a swimsuit for average or oversized women than one for a size-zero model.

Brian Smith, founder of UGG, told me that when he first started the business, he used professional models to portray surfers wearing the company's boots. Smith quickly realized this was not the most effective approach. "None of the real surfers I found wanted to be associated with the original ads because they were fake and trying to create an image," Smith said. So he started using real photos of actual up-and-coming young surfers on real beaches, which made all the difference. "The young kids reading these magazines were dying to be on the beaches where the photographs were taken," he pointed out. "The essence of good advertising is figuring out how to turn on your consumer."

For another clear example of how much millennials value authenticity, let's look again at the popularity of Snapchat. I asked a group of people thirty-five years or older, "What is the first thing that comes to mind when you hear about millennials using Snapchat?" Almost all of them said something along the lines of Snapchat being an easier way to send naked pictures. This is unfortunate. People fail to realize the true value of Snapchat. It provides a great opportunity for organizations of all sizes and even personal brands.

Unlike other social media platforms, it is very difficult to be inauthentic on Snapchat because it covers every aspect of communication. For example, people often complain that you can't communicate emotions in a text because you can't hear the other person's voice or see their face and body language. Snapchat has solved that issue. When you send a Snapchat message, you get to see the person's face, whether it be a photo or video. You can see if s/he is saying something sarcastically or sincerely. If you don't want to record a video, you can just send a quick one-line text with a photo.

The experience is different on Facebook, Twitter, and Instagram. On each of these platforms, you get to edit your message and picture to make everything much more glamorous than it actually is. You can edit every picture you post. You can edit every message you publish. Snapchat has filters, but you cannot enhance the photo to make yourself look skinnier, make the grass brighter and the sky bluer, or make your teeth sparkling white (just brush your teeth, it's not that hard). You cannot crop someone out of a photo. This brings a very authentic vibe to every interaction.

The "Stories" feature on Snapchat allows you to send the same message to all your friends who use the app. The popular Miami-based music producer DJ Khaled has used this feature to build his brand.

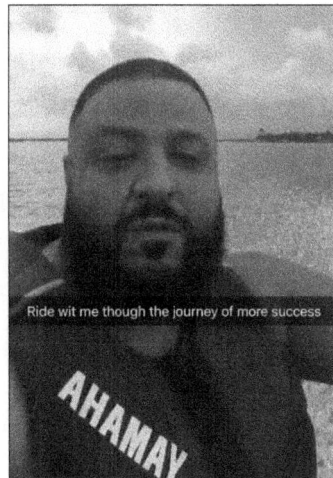
Ride wit me though the journey of more success
AHAMAY

It provides an authentic way to inform his followers about his day-to-day life. Snapchat provides up-to-date, insightful information, and it does not clog people's news feeds or get annoying. You decide exactly when you want to look at people's stories.

Another important aspect for companies to recognize is that millennials want to feel a personal connection with a brand. They do not just want to know the quality and price of a product or service. Because of this, companies should start functioning more like media outlets. They should be constantly pumping out content. They should do this not only to brand themselves but to also provide value to their community.

One of my favorite brands is Chubbies. It makes men's shorts with a five-and-a-half-inch inseam, as opposed to the standard eleven- to nine-inch inseam that most men wear. The company was started by four guys from San Francisco who all attended Stanford together. They wanted to re-create the men's short shorts that were popular in the 1970s and 1980s (yup, this is all your fault, baby boomers). After seeing the trends of loud colors, crazy patterns, and different fabrics, they launched their company and marketed their shorts to millennials, specifically fraternity brothers and those who want to have a great time every second of every day.

The reason I love Chubbies so much isn't because I can show off my thighs. It isn't even because of the quality of the product. It's because the company blows my mind with how it markets itself. Chubbies nails all the points that are crucial to building a brand that millennials love. It has established a strong sense of community, value to the consumers, and interaction with customers. Chubbies promotes its brand as a lifestyle and not just a product. Rather than directly selling its product, it indirectly sells it through the content it posts on social media.

Let me break that down for you. First and most important is creating a sense of community. As I mentioned before, brands that thoroughly understand every aspect of their target market have a huge advantage. Chubbies understands what its customers are doing, thinking, eating, listening to, and watching. Building a community is so simple once you sufficiently understand your target market. You can interact with them, they will interact with you, and they will start to see you as a friend and not just a brand.

Having an active community is important, but brands must be careful not to just pump out content that is directly about the brand. Instead, they need to provide value to their customers beyond just discounts. For example, Chubbies provides humor in its content. It may sound strange, but this is value, whether you think of it that way. When a consumer is able to laugh at content and then share it with friends who also find it funny, it gradually builds a community. One by one, people will share, like, and retweet content with their friends.

Of course, many brands can't rely on humor as a value proposition in their content. If you're marketing a sports-related product, then your added value might be facts and statistics geared toward the sports-loving community. If you're marketing a food-based brand, you might create content consisting of recipes, baking suggestions, and photos showcasing creative uses of your product.

All of this may seem obvious, but it's not. Yes, it's obvious that companies have to understand their target market. But many times, they fail to fully understand their potential costumers inside and out. By producing content that is strictly customized for their specific community, companies have countless opportunities to grow their brand and increase sales.

I genuinely believe that if brands stick with being authentic and incorporate everything discussed above into their content, they will be able to dramatically increase sales. Some brands scream at their community, "COME BUY NOW!" or "CLICK THE LINK BELOW TO START SHOPPING TODAY!" This is not authenticity. On the contrary, marketers must learn to naturally integrate value into the content they are producing, and that content will do its magic.

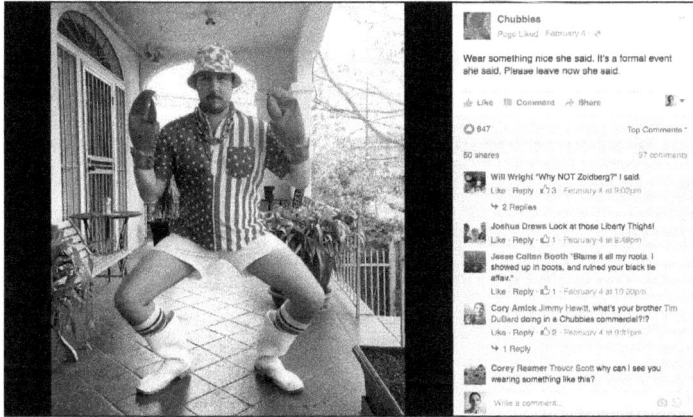

This is definitely one of the main reasons that Chubbies has been so successful with millennials. It uses fun, quirky, and relatable content as a means to drive sales. By following Chubbies' lead and posting authentic photos or videos of customers using their product or service, companies stand a better chance of connecting with millennials.

The picture above is an example, one of hundreds, from Chubbies' Facebook account. As a customer, I see that the guy in this picture doesn't seem to care what others think of him. He's the life of the party, he likes to stand out, and he loves to just have fun. I can relate to every aspect of this picture, and now that I relate to it on a personal level, I am much more inclined to buy the product as well as share, like, and comment on the post.

The key to creating a brand enjoyed by millennials is to provide extra value beyond what simply comes with a purchase. Again, Chubbies nails this one, and it's another reason why millions of other millennials and I love them so much. For example, at different times of the year, Chubbies has online events where it includes various different products in addition to your main purchase. If you buy a pair of shorts, you may also get a free flag, tank top, hat, or Croakies sunglass straps. It includes its world-famous content with these products, which makes consumers laugh and smile, and provides another marketing opportunity for its brand.

Millennials want people to market to them in language they see as authentic. Millennials do not always use the cleanest language. We often tend to use curse words in our day-to-day life. We've grown up with cursing, nudity, and provocative actions all around us in the media we consume.

Like I said before, companies need to be aware of this phenomenon so that they can use it to their advantage. Some companies have used this kind of language very effectively in their marketing. For example, in 2014, Kmart launched a marketing campaign called Ship My Pants. For starters, I found this hilarious and very unexpected. I had to rewind the TV commercial several times to figure out if they were saying "ship" or "shit."

Kmart understood that millennials would find this funny. Many young people loved the ad campaign and shared it with others, creating a viral sensation that did Kmart's marketing for it. So what's my advice to brands that want to tap into the millennial generation but don't want to curse? Take a risk. Rather than safely sticking to more traditional marketing strategies, don't be afraid to try something with a bit more edge. Don't be nervous about what might happen to your brand.

When attempting to appeal to millennials, companies should not act like marketers. They should act more like friends. Part of this is using the same language as millennials. However, this doesn't mean just using curse words.

Smart marketers also understand the slang being used by their target audience. In Philadelphia and surrounding areas like New York City, many people use the word *jawn*. It's used every day as a noun to describe almost anything. Urbandictionary.com defines *jawn* as, "A word used by Philly cats to describe anything and everything. New York City cats interject with the word 'joint,' but it doesn't convey the same feelings. 'You see that car? That jawn was hot.'"

All my friends and most other high schoolers use this word, or at least know what it means. By using this word in their advertising, some Philadelphia companies are attracting a lot of millennial customers. For example, a particular pizza joint may set itself apart as being more hip than others simply by using the word *jawn* in its ads. Companies can grow their brand by using slang words that millennials use. However, they also need to be aware that slang changes from area to area, which is another reason why it's so important to thoroughly understand each specific market.

GoPro is another company that markets brilliantly to millennials. GoPro does not post traditional promotional ads directing customers to its website, yet as of May 2016, it has close to nine million followers on Instagram. Early on in its marketing, GoPro effectively established that its cameras are for adventurous people who hike, travel, skydive, surf, and do other outdoor activities. Users are able to capture all this action from a first-person point of view on their GoPro camera.

Every day, GoPro posts several photos submitted by users. It never posts a picture taken on an iPhone or a professional camera—only the highest quality pictures taken on a GoPro. In this way, its customers get to participate in the company's marketing. It helps GoPro, and it allows its customers to feel like a part of the community.

The company receives thousands of photos a day from GoPro users atop the Grand Canyon, surfing the Atlantic, or climbing Mount Everest. Each photo is a testimonial for the company. The company has never forced the users to do anything; people just want their pictures on GoPro's Instagram site.

Creating a sense of community with the target market is vital if a brand hopes to flourish. One important way to do this is by interacting with customers. Unfortunately, many companies are not interacting with their community. For instance, they fail to respond to comments their customers post online. They are not taking full advantage of social media.

No matter how negative a comment or question may be, the company should address it. If someone sees a Chipotle ad on his/her Facebook feed and then leaves a comment asking if s/he might get $E. coli$ from eating there, Chipotle should respond. It may not always be pleasant, but it is important because it shows that the brand cares about its customers, and it's not just using social media to generate more sales. One potential customer contacted Chipotle with a concern about $E. coli$ in the restaurant's food. If the company fails to address his concern, it may not only lose him as a customer, but it could also lose anyone he's friends with on Facebook.

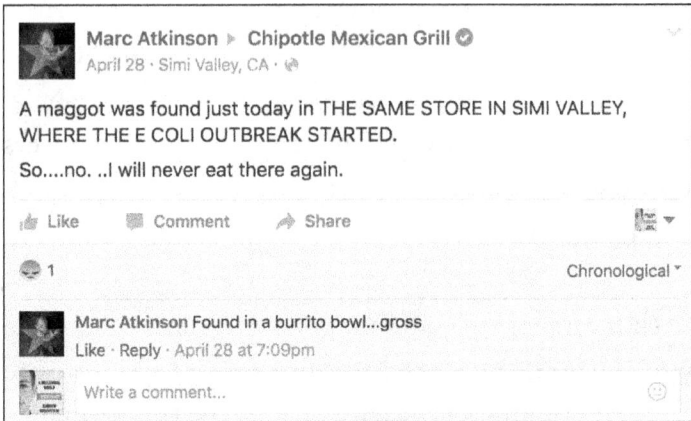

> **Marc Atkinson** ▶ Chipotle Mexican Grill ✓
> April 28 · Simi Valley, CA · ⊜
>
> A maggot was found just today in THE SAME STORE IN SIMI VALLEY,
> WHERE THE E COLI OUTBREAK STARTED.
> So....no. ..I will never eat there again.
>
> 👍 Like   💬 Comment   ↗ Share   ▾
>
> 😑 1   Chronological ▾
>
> **Marc Atkinson** Found in a burrito bowl...gross
> Like · Reply · April 28 at 7:09pm
>
> Write a comment...   ☺

Companies should take advantage of negative comments
because they provide valuable feedback. One negative comment is not such a big deal, but multiple negative comments
can help them understand what they are doing wrong and
how to address it. By doing this, companies will not only be
providing value to the people buying their product, but they
will also be building their community. Customers feel like
they are being listened to, as opposed to just talking to an
anonymous customer service person behind a desk giving
the same answer to everyone. Businesses should promote
that sense of interaction between the company and the
customer so that the customer keeps wanting to come back.

Last year, I bought tickets to Budweiser's Made in America Festival. Budweiser did a great job of interacting with
its community during the festival. Whenever someone

commented on a Facebook photo or tweet, Budweiser immediately responded. Among other information, it told people how to acquire tickets and gave directions to the festival. The company provided value to every person. By interacting with its consumers, it came across as authentic.

Again, it is very important for companies to connect with their customers on a personal level. Beyond just being the company you buy your socks from, or the company that's putting on a music festival you're going to attend, they should also provide value by answering questions, giving tips, and helping build a sense of community.

There is such a thing now as "old school" social media. Of course, many people have used cell phones and personal computers since the early 1990s. Previous generations were able to call customer service on the phone. They were able to use the Internet to find information. Millennials, though, grew up with media that is far more interactive.

Today, you can post a comment or question on Facebook, Twitter, reddit, or another platform and get real feedback from different perspectives. Whether you are a company, a celebrity, or just promoting your personal brand, you can instantly reach a wide variety of ages, races, and genders. Millennials have grown up in this diverse, interactive environment. Companies hoping to reach millennials must understand this and also learn to be interactive. They must find ways to make us part of the conversation.

Somewhat surprisingly, one company that is successfully engaging its community is Oreo. From an e-commerce perspective, Oreo is probably not going to sell many cookies online, but it has brilliantly realized that people are not just eating its cookies. Customers are finding other creative uses for the product, like cooking and cake decorating.

The company has effectively used social media to take advantage of this fact. Every day, Oreo posts new recipes, whether it be an Oreo cake, frosting, or mixture of cookie crumbles and cherry nuts. Users interact with the company online every day. Oreo is part of the conversation because it understands its target market of people who love to experiment with food.

Another company that cleverly uses social media, specifically Twitter, is Denny's. Denny's understands what the day-to-day life of its target market looks like, and it incorporates this into its Twitter marketing. For example, on December 5, 2015, it posted a tweet saying, "It's Saturday night. The club can wait. Where are the chicken strips?"

Let's break that down. It's Saturday night. Denny's understands its target market are millennials going out to clubs, partying, and drinking. Those people are going to get hungry. Not once did Denny's say, "Before you go to the club, come to Denny's to get your chicken strips!" Instead, it simply promoted its product by incorporating it into the lifestyle of its target market.

Denny's also knows the importance of timing its advertisements. Some argue that timing doesn't matter for Twitter, Instagram, and other platforms. As long as you target the right audience, you'll get the proper response. I disagree. I believe timing is a crucial factor.

For example, Denny's posted its tweet at 4:30 p.m., right when people are starting to get hungry and make their dinner plans. As a result, it got more than 11,000 retweets and 13,000 favorites. If Denny's had posted its tweet at 8:00 a.m., it would not have gotten the same response. By timing its tweet wisely, though, the response was overwhelming.

This provides a clear example of effective timing, understanding the target market, and always being immersed in your community. It is understanding what your company is, who your target market is, and what times they are most likely going to act on what you want them to do. If Denny's wants its customers to buy chicken strips, it should not be posting at 10:00 p.m. when people are already drunk at the club. It should be posting before people go out.

In this social media age, it is vital for companies to constantly release new content in order to keep their customers in conversation. Content is key. Content is what's going to drive sales. You may not see an immediate direct link between content and sales, but you are going to see it when your target audience starts interacting, and you're getting more likes on your social media platforms.

From my perspective, getting a hundred likes on your Facebook page is more important than making ten sales. It is more valuable in the sense that you are going to be growing a community of fans who love and talk about your product. This, of course, will ultimately translate to future sales.

The chief marketing officer of a Fortune 500 company once asked author Gary Vaynerchuk about the value of using social media for her business. What was the real return on investment of social media? "I don't mean to offend you, and this isn't a joke," Gary said. "But let me ask you this. What is the return on investment of your mother?"

Gary pointed out that there is no way to qualify all the value you receive from your mother. When you were about to get a mullet haircut in fifth grade, maybe she saved you embarrassment by recommending against it. Maybe she helped you build a toy rocket and win the eighth-grade science project. One day, she may give a speech at your wedding.

You will never be able to adequately quantify a return on investment for everything your mother does for you.

Using social media to grow your business is similar. You may never see the exact return on investment, but it goes beyond just sales. You will see the return when you are growing your community of customers and fans. Therefore, companies hoping to reach millennials should continue investing in social media marketing and doing it on a much more personal level.

As I said before, we are living in a millennial world. Hopefully, what we've discussed in this book will enable you to better understand who we are, how we think and operate, and what we have to offer. We are more connected, diverse, and interactive than any generation in history. Many of us have an entrepreneurial spirit that compels us to identify problems and find solutions.

When we put our minds to it, even something like a learning disability cannot prevent us from achieving success. In fact, it only makes us work harder in pursuit of our goals. Personally, I hate when someone tells me I don't have a shot, or that traditional school is the only path to success. As I work to achieve my dreams, I may encounter a hundred "nos," but it will only drive me that much harder to get a "yes."

I am a millennial. I cannot be defined by a random Google search or negative media depictions of my generation. We are much more powerful than that. We possess boundless potential. We have a desire to improve the world, along with the passions and strengths to make it happen.

Whether you are a millennial, a company trying to connect with us, or someone from a different generation, we can all work together to improve one another's lives and make a positive impact on the world. So now that you know us a little better, what are we waiting for? Let's get started.

ACKNOWLEDGMENTS

WOW! Where do I start? I really don't think I would be here if it weren't for the most amazing parents in the whole world. Mom, although you questioned every word, picture, and punctuation mark in this book, you have been a huge part in my life while writing it as well as the past few years of this crazy ride. You taught me that questioning situations inside and out is the best way to make something as perfect as possible—and that lesson is one of the many reasons why I love you. I can't say it enough: Thank you. To Dad, you are one the coolest guys in the world, and you never fail to impress me. My entire entrepreneurial mind-set and spirit comes from you and the rich business history your family has instilled in you that you have passed down to me. Thank you for everything, and I love you so much.

To Adam, my best friend since before I can remember, thank you for always making me laugh and for making me realize that I shouldn't care what others think of me—a lesson that I provide to millennials in this book that I think everyone should learn! I love you, and I appreciate all of your support over the years.

To Bubbie, thank you for being one of my biggest fans. I can always count on you to give me honest feedback from one of the smartest people I know! I love you so, so much and appreciate everything you have done for me.

To Oma and Grandpa, thank you for instilling in me the entrepreneurial mind-set that both of you have. From traveling halfway around the world with me and telling me old stories about when you were younger to taking walks on the beach, both of you have made a significant impact on my life and the way that I look at the world.

To all of my aunts and uncles who have gone out of their way to support me in any way possible: I love you guys and appreciate everything each and every one of you have done for me, no matter how big or how small it has been. I love you all: Aunt Shelly, Uncle Tony, Aunt Stacey, Aunt Jeanine, Aunt Ilene, Uncle Harlan, and Aunt Melanie.

To my amazing cousins, who have all been interested in everything I have done, for giving an endless amount of support, and for just being the most loving and caring people I can ask for: Sam, Noah, and little Jordyn.

To my best friends, who are always cheering me on and always inspiring me to do more and more. I can't express how much each one of you has impacted my life; thank you so much. To Tyler Goldman, from growing up, constantly fighting (you always winning), and talking for hours about anything and everything to hanging at the shore during the warm summer days, you are my best friend, and I love you. Thank you for always supporting me and trusting me in whatever I decide to do. To Paige Betoff, for being the smartest and funniest friend anyone could ever have. It doesn't matter where we are, you never fail to impress me. I can't even tell you how much the support you have given me has meant. Thank you for being there for me. And to every single one of my best friends from school and the neighborhood to camp, and to everyone who has supported me: I appreciate it.

To Daniel Fine, for being a best friend, older brother, mentor, boss, and everything in between. You took a chance with me as a summer intern, and ever since that day, you have trusted me to be the youngest employee in your company. I appreciate everything you have taught me. This book has many stories that you and I both experienced and lessons that you have instilled in me because you saw something in me that others didn't.

To Rich Sedmak, PJ Raduta, and Scott Aronow, thank you

for being the first to teach me what it takes to be an entrepreneur and how to run a business with whatever money, products, and services I have. All of you have challenged me to think outside of the box in every situation and instilled in me that no matter what "it" is, I either have to do "it" better than the rest or create/provide something that no one else has done.

To Pat Roberts and Nancy Blair, this book would have never even be a thought without the amazing institution you founded ten years ago, a place that I gladly call home: AIM Academy. The tremendous support you have given me is outstanding and means the world to me. AIM is the reason I can write, read, have my passion of entrepreneurship, and so much more. I can't thank you both enough for the amazing school you welcomed me into six years ago.

To the greatest teachers I ever had—Beau Martin, Carolyn Bjornson, Alli Gubanich, Jesse Korff, Jenna Bonshock, and Chris Herman: Thank you for challenging me in every aspect of my life and not only teaching me in the classroom, but for making me think in different and creative ways outside of the classroom. You allowed me to fail and helped me realize what it is that I need to do that will make me be as close to perfect, no matter the situation.

To Sophia Gross, the greatest friend and business partner

anyone could ask for: You and I have had some of the most amazing memories together—from speaking in front of thousands of people and designing shirts for Opportunity Rise at 3:00 a.m. to learning what it takes to run a non-profit at such a young age. Everything you and I have done together will be memories I'll remember for the rest of my life. I love you and thank you for everything you have done with me for many years.

To Kyle Petras for doing an amazing job on my cover photo! You are constantly impressing me with your creativity. Keep up the amazing work!

And finally, a thank you to...you! I appreciate your taking the time to read something that I put blood, sweat, and tears into. I believe this book has the power to change the way you look at millennials or, if you are a millennial, the way that you live your life. *A Millennial World* is something I believe in strongly. Without millennials in the workplace, companies that want to become the innovators and leaders of the marketing world and target the most significant audience for their brands will face many issues in the coming years. I hope you enjoy the book just as much as I did writing it.

ABOUT THE AUTHOR

ANDREW ROSENSTEIN is a 17-year-old entrepreneur in Philadelphia, Pennsylvania. After being diagnosed with dyslexia at age 12, Rosenstein wanted to change misperceptions about people with learning disabilities. In 2012, as a seventh grader at AIM Academy, a college prep school for students with language-based learning disabilities, Rosenstein launched his first e-commerce business. He sold peoples' "trash" (unwanted valuables such as electronics, handbags, and shoes) online, taking 30 percent for his services and giving the customer 70 percent. After generating nearly $20,000 in revenue, he felt compelled to start a business that meant more to him personally.

In 2013, along with his friend Sophia Gross, Rosenstein started Opportunity Rise, a student-led organization that raises awareness and funding for students with learning disabilities. Opportunity Rise sells branded apparel, with part of the proceeds, enabling Andrew and Sophia to give talks around the U.S., sharing the message that having a learning disability can be an advantage rather than a disadvantage.

In 2014, while expanding Opportunity Rise, Rosenstein secured a summer internship at Glass-U, a millennial-led company that markets customizable sunglasses. Having worked his way up from an intern who sold sunglasses at street shows and college campuses, he now manages the company's social media marketing efforts.

In 2015, Rosenstein spent a summer in London, England, working for several companies that focus on marketing to the millennial generation. This experience further ignited his passion for entrepreneurship and learning how to effectively market products and services for millennials.

Rosenstein has spoken at length on the topics he discusses in *A Millennial World*, including the President's Lunch at Global Business Group in New York, YMS London in 2015 and 2016, and time spent as a TEDx Speaker.

In addition to being a full-time student, varsity basketball player, and managing his business ventures, Rosenstein travels around the country, sharing his research, insights, and personal experiences on the power and potential of millennials. He has spoken at many venues, including the International Dyslexia Association, Dr. Angela Duckworth's Character Lab, and University of Pennsylvania's Positive Psychology Center.

BOOK
— IN A —
BOX

IT'S TIME TO WRITE YOUR BOOK

"My experience with Book In A Box was outstanding! When I first had the dream of writing a book, I never knew how much work it actually took. But after working with such a wonderful team of editors, designers, and publishing managers, they helped me out, and all I had to do was talk about what I loved and I what I wanted the book to be about."

— ANDREW ROSENSTEIN

Andrew is a seventeen-year-old entrepreneur with multiple businesses and success stories under his belt. He's been able to do anything he set his mind to, but that means he didn't have time to sit at a keyboard for a year to put his thoughts on paper.

So Andrew took his own advice and sought the best way to accomplish his goal of writing a book. As a millennial himself, his use of Book In A Box is just another example of leveraging the right resources to get the job done.

Book In A Box is a company that turns ideas into books.

We surround our authors with a team of publishing professionals who help clarify and structure their book idea, get their words out of their head (in their voice), and then professionally publish their book, in about ten times less time than if they do it themselves.

Andrew used us for the book you have in your hands.

If you have valuable ideas in your head as well and believe they might make a good book, we're happy to talk and see if we can help.

Start here: www.bookinabox.com/AndrewRosenstein

www.ingramcontent.com/pod-product-compliance
Lightning Source LLC
Chambersburg PA
CBHW071602200326
41519CB00021BB/6840